Unbelievable Pictures and Facts About Anteaters

By: Olivia Greenwood

Introduction

Anteaters are very unique animals, they even look unique. They are very fascinating animals and today is your day to learn all about them.

How long do baby anteaters remain with their mothers for?

Baby anteaters usually remain with their mothers for up to two years.

Do anteaters have long or short noses?

Anteaters are very recognizable as they have very long noses.

How many babies do the female anteater have each year?

Believe it or not, female anteaters only have one baby each year.

What is the name of baby anteater?

The name for a baby anteater is a pup.

What are many anteaters together called?

Even though anteaters prefer being alone, they do gather in groups during mating time. Groups of anteaters together are known as a parade.

Can anteaters be trained to be tame?

Surprisingly the answer is a big yes, anteaters can actually be trained to be tame.

Are these animals aggressive ones?

In general, anteaters are not aggressive animals, although they can become fierce, especially if they feel threatened.

How do anteaters protect themselves from threats?

As it was previously mentioned anteaters do not have teeth so they are unable to bite. In order to protect themselves, they make use of their claws which are extremely sharp.

Are anteaters social animals or not?

Unlike some animals, anteaters are not social animals, they prefer to be alone.

Do anteaters have good or bad eyesight?

Anteaters have a tendency to have really bad eyesight and they are unable to see in the dark at all.

What type of places do anteaters live?

The anteater is able to adapt well to many different environments. They can be found in forests, rainforests, trees and even near water.

Are these animals nocturnal or not?

Anteaters are nocturnal animals, which means that they sleep during the day time and they are wide awake at night.

Are these animals messy or tidy eaters?

Most animals are usually very messy eaters but for some reason, anteaters are extremely tidy eaters, they don't make any mess at all.

How many years do anteaters live for on average?

Anteaters can live up until different ages, it depends on the exact species and if they live in the wild or not. Although on average they live up till around 14 years.

What is the length of their tongues?

Anteaters have extremely long sticky tongues, which are very thin and can go up to 2 feet in length.

Are anteaters carnivores or herbivores?

Anteaters are actually carnivores they feed on ants and other types of insects such as termites.

How many teeth do anteaters have?

This is actually a trick question because anteaters have no teeth at all. They are edentate which means that they have absolutely no teeth, not even one.

What part of the world do these anteaters live in?

Anteaters usually can be found in Central America as well as South America, although they can be found in other places too.

How many unique species of anteaters are there?

There are four different types of anteaters.

Which animal group does the anteater fit into?

The anteater fits into the group of animals known as mammals, which are warm-blooded.

CPSIA information can be obtained
at www.ICGtesting.com
Printed in the USA
LVHW071941141019
634123LV00001B/175/P